Bobi y Cuqui en español

Chistes y aventuras del dúo canino

Rita Wirkala

Ilustraciones:

Marcelo Basilio

All Bilingual Press
www.allbilingual.com

Published by All Bilingual Press
Seattle, WA

Copyright © 2021 by All Bilingual Press

All Rights Reserved
Copies may be reproduced by classroom teachers for classroom use only. No part of this publication may be reproduced for storage in a retrieval system without the prior written permission of the publisher. Reproduction of these materials for an entire school or school district is strictly prohibited.

All Bilingual Press
www.allbilingual.com

ISBN: 978-1-7350932-4-6

Printed in USA

Dedico este libro a mis nietas y nietos Livia, Ada, Leia, Desmond y Oliver, quienes siempre celebran los chistes de su "Abu".

I dedicate this book of jokes to my grandchildren Livia, Ada, Leia, Desmond and Oliver, who always celebrate their "Abu's" jokes.

Parte I

Las aventuras de Bobi y Cuqui

ÍNDICE

Parte I. Las aventuras de Bobi y Cuqui, *1*

Parte II. Los chistes de Bobi y Cuqui, *15*

Más sobre perros, *32*

Más chistes, *33*

Traducciones, *34*

CONTENIDO GRAMATICAL

1. *Bobi y Cuqui van al parque.* Verbo "ir". Verbos "gustar" y similares.
2. *La falta sal.* Para expresar posesión. Verbo "faltar".
3. *Cuqui no sabe leer.* Uso del infinitivo. Verbo "doler".
4. *No te va a gustar.* Más usos del infinitivo.
5. *Adivinanza.* Verbos con cambio de raíz (ie, ue, i).
6. *La higiene canina.* Verbos en forma reflexiva y no reflexiva.
7. *¡Buen trabajo, Bobi!* Uso de los pronombres de objeto directo.
8. *¡Cuántas órdenes!* Mandatos afirmativos y negativos.
9. *El más perfecto.* Verbos en el pretérito.
10. *Ayer.* Más verbos en el pretérito. Formas irregulares.
11. *Super perro.* Verbos en el pretérito y el imperfecto.

Bobi y Cuqui van al parque

Continúa en la siguiente página...

cosas = *things*	hay = *there is/are*	comer = *to eat*	cavar = *to dig*	manzana = *apple*
comida = *food*	hueso = *bone*	allí = *there*	¿ves? = *do you see?*	adentro = *inside*

me parece = *it seems to me*
no me gustan = *I don't like it*
a mí también = *me too*
un ratón = *a mouse*
me dan pena = *I pity them*
di = *tell*

oye = *listen*
lugar = *place*
jamón = *ham*
vivo = *ham*
alive = *something*
asco = *disgust*

verdad = *truth*
hambre = *hunger*
no me importa = *I don't care*
queso = *cheese*   me encantan = *I like*
¿qué te pasa? = *what's the matter?*
¿y qué? = *so what?*
me caen mal = *they scare you*

Le falta sal

mira = *look* salsicha = *sausage* sobre = *on* dueño = *owner* trae = *bring*
leyendo = *reading* corre = *run* no puedo = *I can't* derecha = *right*
me duele = *it hurts me* pata = *paw* no te creo = *I don't believe you*
no importa = *it doesn't matter* es mía = *it's mine* qué pena = *too bad*
le falta = *it's lacking* sal = *salt*

Cuqui no sabe leer

cocinando = *cooking* puedes = *can you / you can* saltar = *to jump* todavía = *still*
fuera = *out* toma = *take that* a ver = *let's see*
se dejan de = *stop (doing something)* molestar = *bother* tiene gusto a = *it tastes like*
frijoles = *beans* leer = *to read* cierto = *true* lata = *can*

No te va a gustar...

un poco = *a little*   no te va a gustar = *you are not going to like it*   nada = *nothing*
carne = *meat*   más tarde = *later*   compartir = *to share*   pedazo = *piece*
conmigo = *with me*

Adivinanza

escuchar = *to listen*   adivinanza = *riddle*   dime = *tell me*   dormir (**du**ermer) = *to sleep*
día = *day*   noche = *night*   sale = *goes out*   me refiero = *I refer*
pelo = *hair*   cuerpo = *body*   pista = *hint*   perseguir (*persigue*) = *to chase*
ratones = *mice*   rata = *rat*   siente miedo = *feels fear*   piensa = *think*
vecino = *nehghbor*

continúa....

dame = *give me*   otra = *another*   soñar (sueña) = *to dream*   nobre = *name*
foca = *seal*   claro por eso = *because of this*   nunca = *never*   vienen = *they come*
por aqui = *around here*   empieza = *begins*   vienen= *they come*   por aqui = *around here*

La higiene canina

a mí me bañan = *they bathe me*
a ti te bañan? = *do they bathe you?*
secador = *(hair) dryer*
dientes = teeth
solo = *by myself*

todos los meses = *every month*
yo me baño = *I bathe myself*
casa = *home / house*
secar = *to dry*

¡Buen trabajo, Bobi!

buen trabajo = *good job*   pisos = *floors*   poner la mesa = *to set the table*
quitar = *to clear (the table) / to remove*   regar (**rie**ga) = *to water*

¡Cuántas órdenes!

órdenes = *orders* ven = *come*
ensuciar = *to soil, to get something dirty*
pórtate bien = *behave yourself*
¿entendido? = *understood?*

no vengas = *don't come* mojado = *wet*
no te enojes = *don't get angry*
no hagas = *don't do* agujeros = *holes*

un abrazo = *a hug*
anteojos = *glasses*
ahora = *now*

pero = *but*
no me des = *don't give me*
roncar = *to snore*

romper = *to break*
lengua = *tongue*

El más perfecto

comenzó = *began* primero = *first* cayó = *fell* formó = *formed*
después = *afterwards* mandó = *sent* Dios = *God* nacieron = *they were born*
rayo = *ray* células = *cells* vida = *life* escuché decir = *I hear that*
vinieron = *they came* tierra = *Earth* de todos = *of all* llegó = *arrived*

Ayer

ayer = *yesterday*
fui = *I went*
pantalones = *pants*
sombrero = *hat*
fuimos = *we went*
zapatos = *shoes*
agua = *water*

no viniste = *you didn't come*
tienda = *shop*
de compras = *shopping*
hacer = *to do*
poner = *to put, to put on*
traer = *to bring*
le traje = *I brought him/her*

jugar = *to play*
compramos = *we bought*
comprar = *to buy*
hicieron = *you (all) did*
se puso = *she put on*
me trajo = *she brought me*
ratón = *mouse*

Super-perro

pasó = *happened*   anoche = *last night*
no había nadie = *there was no one*   de repente = *suddenly*
llevaba = *he was wearing (carried)*   oscuros = *dark*
boca = *mouth*   cara = *face*   iba a atacarme = *was going to attack me*
salieron = *they left*   los mordiste = *you bit them*

Yo estaba = *I was*
ventana = *window*
traía = *had*

me desperté = *I woke up*

Parte II

Los chistes de Bobi y Cuqui

La casa blanca

La vacuna

al final = *at the end*   calle = *street*   necesita = *needs*   vacuna = *vaccine*
agarrar = *to get, grab*   chiste = *joke*   ya lo conozco = *I already know it*

Equilibrio 1

El olor

equilibrio = *balance*   levantar = *to raise / lift*   me caigo = *I fall down*
cuál = *which*   olor = *smell*   favorito = *favorite*   pescado = *fish*
tuyo = *yours*   medias sucias = *dirty socks*   mi amo = *my master*

Grande y pequeño

¿Sabes? = *do you know?* le dice = *says to him/her*   cabeza = *head*
cintura = *waist* pequeño/a = *small*

Las Estaciones

estación = *season* or *station*   primavera = *Spring*   flores = *flowers*   escalera = *ladder*
viajar = *to travel*   te subes = *you go up*   notas altas = *high notes*
ladrar = *to bark*

Saltando

Estornudando

saltando = *jumping*
estornudando = *sneezing*
¿cómo así? = *what (do you) mean?*

fácil = *easy*
humanos = *human beings*
no entiendo = *I don't understand*

árboles = *trees*

Extraplanetario

La memoria

tanto = *so much*
lejos = *far*
esconder = *to hide*

tierra = *soil / Earth*
memoria = *memory*
no te preocupes = *don't worry*

marte = *Mars*
recuerdo = *I remember*
va a pasar = *it will pass*

Los trabajos

La foto

hace = *does* abeja = *bee* miel = *honey* trabajador/a = *hard worker*
pez = *fish* nadar = *to swim* nada = *nothing* perezoso = *lazy*
relámpago = *lightning* descarga eléctrica = *electric shock* cielo = *sky* foto = *picture*

Las noticias

Equilibrio 2

noticia = *news* para ti = *for you* albóndigas de carne = *meatballs*
mala = *bad* me levanto = *I get up, I lift myself* me caigo = *I fall down*

Los planetas

La ortografía

¿tú conoces? = *do you know?* claro = *of course* antes = *before* lunes = *Monday*
¿cómo se escribe? = *how do you write?* hache = *H* no se pronuncia = *is not pronounced*
¿se come? = *does one eat it? is it edible?*

Las lunas

Para escribir y para comer

tú, que lo sabes todo = *you, who know everything*   lunas = *moons*   luna llena = *full moon*
luna nueva = *new moon*   cuarta menguante = *waning moon*
cuarta creciente = *waxing moon*   te falta una = *you're missing one*
la medialuna = *the croissant* (called 'the half moon')   griega = *Greek*   gelatina = *gelatine*

Aprendiendo

Toda la familia

aprendiendo = *learning* sé = *I know* escribir = *to write* impresionante = *impressive*
todavía = *still, yet* leer = *to read* conozco = *I know* pulga = *flea* más que tú = *more than you*
tía = *aunt* pulguitas = *little fleas* panza = *belly*

Patos y patas

Resultados...

patos = *ducks*   contar = *to count*   a ver = *let's see*   laguna = *lagoon*
patas = *female ducks (or) paws*   cae = *falls*   pozo = *well*   sale = *gets out*

Transporte público

La otra luna

esquina = *corner*   esperando = *waiting*   demora = *delays*
nueva = *new*   se fue = *it left, went away*   vieja = *old*   llena = *full*

Arriba y abajo

Las hojas

arriba = *up, on top*   abajo = *down, below*   subir = *to go up*   techo = *roof*
morir de frío = *freeze to death*   ¿qué le pasó? = *what happened to?*   hojas = *leaves or pages*
será porque = *it may be because*   otoño = *autum*

Coincidencias

Los sueños de un perro

coincidencias = *coincidences*
enero = *January*
anoche = *last night*
otra vez = *again*

nacer = *to be born*
mismo día = *the same day*
soñar = *to dream*
siempre = *always*

navidad = *Christmas*
cumpleaños = *birthday*
me daban = *they gave me*
eso = *that*

Los trabajos

La foto

hace = *does*   abeja = *bee*   miel = *honey*   trabajador/a = *hard worker*
pez = *fish*   nadar = *to swim*   nada = *nothing*   perezoso = *lazy*
relámpago = *lightning*   descarga eléctrica = *electric shock*   cielo = *sky*   foto = *picture*

MÁS SOBRE PERROS

¿Cuál es...?

a. ¿Cuál es el perro más religioso?

b. ¿Y el perro más sabroso?

c. ¿Y el más trabajador?

d. ¿Y el más peleador?

e. ¿Y el que sabe más de huesos?

f. ¿Y el más santo?

g. ¿Cuál es la mejor manera de hablarle a un perro rabioso?

a. El pastor alemán.
b. ¡El salchicha!
c. El labrador
d. El boxer
e. El sabueso
f. El San Bernardo
g. ¡Bien de lejos!

sabroso = *tasty*
pastor = *shepherd, which also means church pastor*
alemán = *German*
salchicha = *dachshund;* also salchicha = *sausage*
labrador = *Labrador; also farmer*
peleador = *fighter*
sabueso = *hound dog;* but, hueso = *bone*
manera = *way, manner*
rabioso = *mad, with rabies*
de lejos = *from far away*

MÁS CHISTES

a. ¿Sabes cuál es el eco más chistoso?

b. ¿Por qué el perro entró en la iglesia?

c. ¿Sabes qué le dice un libro de matemáticas al otro?

d. ¿Por qué los elefantes están tan arrugados?

e. ¿Por qué te estás mirando tanto al espejo?

f. ¿Cuál es el peor miedo de una serpiente venenosa?

g. ¿Qué dice la sardina cuando ve a un submarino?

h. Cuanto más seca, más mojada. ¿Qué es?

i. Cuanto más grande, menos hay. ¿Qué es?

j. ¿Cuál es el juguete más egoísta?

a. *La navaja -ja -ja*
b. *Porque la puerta estaba abierta.*
c. *¿Qué problema tienes?*
d. *Porque debe ser muy difícil planchar a un elefante.*
e. *Porque el test del virus dice que yo tengo anticuerpos…y estoy tratando de verlos.*
f. *Morderse la lengua.*
g. *¡Mira, una lata de gente!*
h. *La toalla.*
i. *El agujero*
j. *El yo-yo*

eco = *echo*
arrugado = *wrinkled*
espejo = *mirror*
peor = *worse*
venenoso/a = *poisonous*
menos = *less*
juguete = *toy*
egoista = *selfish*
planchar = *to iron*
anticuerpos = *antibodies*
lata = *can*
gente = *people*
toalla = *towel*
agujero = *hole*

TRANSLATIONS
Part I

1. Bobi and Cuqui go to the park

Where are you going, Bobi?
I am going to the park.
Why are you going to the park?
Because there are many delicious things to eat.
Bobi, where are the good things to eat?
Here, you have to dig, see? As I am digging.
An apple! Ugh, that's not dog food.
What do you want?
I want a bone.
Uff, what a demanding little dog!
Oh, I know where there are a lot of bones. Come. Do you see? There are many bones in there.
We are going to have a feast!
Oops! It seems to me that this is not a place for dogs.
I don't care, I don't like museums.
Do you like ham and cheese sandwiches? I love them.
Me too.
So come on, I know where to find some..
I'm sure there is something here for us.
DUMP
Eeeek!
What's wrong?
A mouse, and it is alive.
So what?
They make me sad (*I feel sorry for them*). They disgust me. And I don't like them.
Tell the truth, you are **scared.**
Hey, let's go to the park. I'm not hungry anymore.

2. It needs salt (literally, it lacks salt)

Look, there is a sausage on the table and the owner is reading.
Run and get that sausage, Bobi.
I can't, my right leg hurts.
I don't believe you. OK, I'll go.
It's mine!

No, it's mine!

What a pity!

It doesn't matter, that sausage needs salt (is lacking salt)

3. Cuqui doesn't know how to read

Look, they are cooking sausages. Can you jump?

No, my leg still hurts.

Well, I'm going to jump.

Get out, dog! Take that, let's see if you stop bothering.

Bobi, this sausage tastes like beans…

Right, can't you read, Cuqui? Look at the can. What does it say?

Vegetarian sausages.

4. You are not going to like it

Bobi, can I eat some of that bone?

No. You won't like it. It doesn't have any meat.

Later on…

Cuqui, can you share that piece of meat with me?

No. You are not going to like it. It has no bone.

5. Riddle

Bobi, do you want to hear a riddle?

Yes, tell me.

It (he/she) sleeps during the day and goes out at night. Who is it?

My master.

No, Bobi, I mean an animal with four legs and with hair all over its body. I'll give you another clue: it chases mice.

The rat?

No, Bobi. Think! It is an animal that is afraid of us.

The neighbor's dog?

No!

Give me another clue. What does it dream about?

Sardines.

A seal!

Of course not, Dog, seals don't have four legs nor long hair. Another clue: the name starts with a "G"*

Oh, I know. Gorilla.

Bobi, gorillas are not afraid of dogs.

Yes, they are. That's why they never come around here.

*Cuqui is thinking about "Gato" (cat)

6. Canine Hygiene

They bathe me every month. Do they bathe you?
No. I bathe by myself, in the street.
They dry me (my fur) with a hair dryer. Do they dry you (your fur) too?
No. I dry myself, at home.
They clean (brush) my teeth. Do they clean (brush) yours, too?
No, I clean (brush) my teeth by myself.

7. Good work, Bobi!

Bobi, who cleans the floors in your house?
My master cleans them.
Who sets the table?
My master sets it.
And who clears it?
I clear it.
Bobi, who waters the plants in your house?
I water them.

8. So many orders!

Bobi, come.
Don't come in all wet.
Don't get my floor dirty. Go outside. Don't be mad, Bobi.
Behave yourself. Be a good dog.
And don't make holes in the garden, understand?
Eat your own food, Bobi, don't eat the cat's food. Give me a hug.
But don't break my glasses.
And don't kiss me with a wet tongue (or, don't lick me).
Now, let's go to sleep, and don't snore!

9. The most perfect

This is how it all began, Cuqui.
All what, Bobi?
Our existence. First, a meteorite that fell on Earth brought the elements. Well, that's what I've heard.
Then, God sent a lightning bolt and electricity formed the first cells of life. Then the plants were born.
Later the animals came.
And finally, the best, the most perfect of all arrived:
THE DOG!

10. Yesterday

Why didn't you come to play yesterday?

Yesterday I went to the store with my master. We bought pants. What did you do?

Oh, I also went shopping. My master bought a hat for herself and I bought one for myself. And what else did you do?

Later, we went home.

She put on tennis shoes and I put on my shoes. Then we went for a run.

In the park she gave (brought) me water. And I gave (brought) her a mouse.

11. Super Dog

Do you know what happened last night?

No, tell me.

It was midnight. I was sleeping. There was no one at home.

Suddenly a man came in through the window. He was small, wearing dark glasses. He had a Bulldog with him.

The dog had a huge mouth and a horrible face.

He was 3 times my size. He was going to attack me when, suddenly, I transformed myself into a Super-Dog.

When they saw me, they both ran off.

And? Didn't you bite them?

No, because then I woke up.

TRANSLATION
Part II

La casa blanca - The White house
Where do you live?
In the white house
In Washington???
NO! In the white house at the end of the street!

La vacuna - The vaccine
Do you know why the computer needs a vaccine?
So as not to catch the virus! (I already know that joke, Bobi ...)

Equilibrio 1 - Balance
Bobi, why are you lifting a leg to pee?
Because if I lift two, I'll fall!

El olor - The smell
What is your favorite smell?
The smell of fish. And yours?
The smell of my master's dirty socks. I love it!

Grande y pequeño - Big and small
Do you know what zero says to nine?
No. What does it say?
What a big head you have!
And do you know what zero says to eight?
No.
What a small waist you have!

Las estaciones - The Seasons*

What is your favorite season, Cuqui? Spring. I love flowers . And yours, Bobi? The train station. I love traveling!

*estación in Spanish is both "season" and "station"

Las notas altas - The high notes

Cuqui, why are you climbing a ladder to bark?
To bark the high notes. I'm a soprano, you know!

Saltando - Jumping

I can jump higher than a tree.
How?
Easy, Cuqui. Trees don't jump ... ha ha ha

Estornudando - Sneezing

Why do humans say cheese, in English, when they sneeze? How is that,
(what do you mean) Bobi?
My master says ¡At cheese!

Extraplanetario - Extraplanetary

Why do you like digging in the dirt* so much?
Well, Mars is too far.

*tierra = means"dirt" and "Earth"

La memoria - Memory

I have a problem with my memory. I don't remember where I hid my bone.
Well, don't worry, Bobi. It will pass. When did this problem start?
What problem?

Los trabajos - Jobs

What does the bee do*, Bobi?
It makes honey. She's very hard-working.
And a fish?
Nothing*. He's a lazy!

*hacer = "to do" or "to make"

nada = "nothing"; also: "he/she swims"

La foto - The picture

Do you know what lightning is, Cuqui?

It's an electrical discharge in the sky.

Noooo, it is God taking pictures of dogs, his most perfect creation!

Las noticias - The news

I have good news and bad news for you.

Tell me the good news first.

I have two delicious meatballs.

And the bad news?

They are already in my stomach.

Equilibrio 2- Balance 2

Look, Bobi, I can stand on two legs.

Look Cuqui, I can stand on three legs. AAAAYYYYYY !! And I fall on all fours!

Los planetas - The planets

Do you know the planets of the solar system, Bobi?

Sure: Mercury, Venus, Mars, Jupiter, Saturn …

And the most important one that comes before Mars*?

Monday!

*martes = Tuesday and also Mars

La ortografía - Spelling

Bobi, do you know how to spell "hueso" (bone) ?

No.

With an "h". But the "h" is not pronounced.

But can you eat it?

Las lunas - The moons

Cuqui, you, who knows everything… Do you know how many moons there are?

Sure. There are four: The full moon, the new moon, the crescent, the waning…

You are missing one.

Which one?

The croissant!

* a croissant is called "media luna" (half a moon) in Spanish

Para escribir y para comer - To write and to eat

In Spanish there are two letters "i", the Greek one (Y), and the Latin one (i). Did you know that?

Yes, and there are also two "G's".

Which ones?

The Latin "G" and the gelatin ... (G-Latin)

Aprendiendo - Learning

Look, I can write.

Impressive. What does it say?

I don't know, I still can't read.

Toda la familia - The whole family

How many animals do you know, Cuqui?

I know the dog, the cat, the mouse and the flea. And you?

Many more than you! I know the dog, the cat, the mouse, the mother flea, the aunt flea, and all the little fleas that live in my fur (my belly).

Patos y patas - Ducks and paws* or male ducks and female ducks

Can you count?

Sure.

Let's see, how many ducks are there in this lagoon?

There are four.

And how many paws *(patas*)*?

There are two.

Don't you know how to multiply, Bobi? There are twelve! (4 + 2) x 2 = 12

"pata" = female duck, and also leg for animals or paws

Resultados - Results

How does a dog come out when it falls into a well?

All wet!

Transporte público - Public transportation

Two fleas are at a bus stop waiting for transport. And one says to the other:

"The dog is so late today!"

La otra luna - The other moon

Today there is a new moon.
Where did the old one go?
There is no old moon, Bobi, there is a full moon.
Full of what?

Arriba y abajo - Above and below

The TV says that the temperature is going up.
Uh-oh! If it goes up to the roof, we'll freeze to death down here!

Las hojas - The leaves*

Bobi, what happened to your master's book? Why did the pages fall out?
I don't know. It might be because Autumn (Fall) is coming.

    * **hojas** in Spanish means both leaves and pages

Coincidencias - Coincidences

What day were you born?
On December 25th. And it's Christmas. What a coincidence, right?
I was born on January 13th. The same day as my birthday. That is more of a coincidence!

Los sueños de un perro - A dog's dreams

Last night I dreamed that they gave me a sausage again.
Do they always give you sausage?
No, I dreamed that again!

El comienzo de todo - The beginning of everything

Bobi, tell me, according to scientists, how did the universe start?
With a "U"?

Pobre sapo… Poor frog…

The lion, King of the jungle, announced:
"I'm going to eat all the small-mouthed animals."
"Ha Ha Ha" laughed the crocodile.
"And then", said the lion, "I'm going to eat the big-mouth animals."
"Oops!" said the crocodile, "puuur tuuud ..."(poor toad)

Más sobre perros- More about dogs

a. What is the most religious dog? *German shepherd*
b. And the tastiest dog? *Salchicha*
c. And the hardest worker? *Labrador*
d. And the best fighter? *Boxer*
e. And the one who knows the most about bones? *Hound dog*
f. And the holiest? *San Bernardo*
g. What's the best way to talk to a mad dog? *From far away*

Más chistes - More jokes

a. Do you know what the funniest echo is?
   The orange-ha-ha-ha-ha-ha
b. Why did the dog enter the church?
   Because the door was open ...
c. Do you know what one math book says to another?
   What's your problem?
d. Why are elephants so wrinkled?
   Because it must be very difficult to iron an elephant!
e. Why are you looking at yourself in the mirror so much?
   Because the virus test says I have antibodies. I'm trying to see them!
f. What is a poisonous snake's worst fear?
   Biting her tongue!
g. What does the sardine say when it sees a submarine?
   Look, a can of people!
h. The more it dries, the wetter it gets. What is it?
   A towel
i. The bigger it is, the less there is. What is it?
   The hole
j. What is the most selfish toy?
   The yo-yo

www.ingramcontent.com/pod-product-compliance
Lightning Source LLC
Chambersburg PA
CBHW042359070526
44585CB00029B/2996